# MORE FANTASTIC WORD PUZZLES

(Original title: Super Word Tricks)

**Compiled by Sonia Black & Pat Brigandi**

SCHOLASTIC INC.
New York Toronto London Auckland Sydney

ISBN 0-590-96225-6

12 11 10 9 8 7 6 5                                              1/0

Printed in the U.S.A.                                              01

# INTRODUCTION
# PLAY
# WORDS

Take a good look at this word puzzle. It represents a familiar phrase. Can you guess what it is? Say out loud exactly what you see. Give up? This word puzzle represents the phrase "play on words!" Get it? Terrific! This super book is packed with word puzzles that are all plays on words. Each puzzle illustrates a familiar word, phrase, or saying. To find the solutions, look *carefully* at how all the letters or symbols in the puzzle are positioned. Some may be backward, forward, up, down, or diagonal. Some letters may be tall, short, broken, or curved. Check out these important clues and more to help you find the answer to each puzzle. Now, are you ready for lots of word puzzle fun? Then let's go. This could be SOMEthing (the start of something big)!

# PEOPLE WATCHING

The following word puzzles are all about people.
Hint: Some are proper names and some are not.

**1**

REVIRDTAES

**2**

*ncle Sam*

**3**

shkinniing argmhotr

**4**

# EMPLOYMENT

# HOROBOD

women women women

**7**

# JOHN silver

**8**

VIOLET

**9**

ALICE

6

10

11

NfrEieEndD

12

M A N

BOARD

13

*OLIVER*

14

**DR.** do

15

Y
Y MEN
Y

bopper

M ^A TOWN ^N

**LABROTHERW**

19

20

RANGER

21

# VA DERS

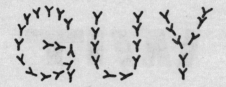

ANTS ANTS ANTS ANTS ANTS
ANTS ANTS ANTS ANTS ANTS

**25**

MOTHER

**26**

WIT

**27**

REK
WALK

12

# WEATHERWISE

The next set of word puzzles are all related to the weather.

## 1

# THE CLO UDS

## 2

$$\frac{0}{10°}$$
$$50°$$

## 3

**4**

DRIZZLE

**5**

SHOWERS

**6**

TEMPERATURE

**7**

# wether

**8**

## THE WEATHER
## A BIT

**9**

*Heat Heat Heat Heat*

# NAME THAT TUNE

Song titles are the subject of the upcoming section.

N
O
T
T
U
B

## YOUR
## COAT

# MY 1111 LIFE

# DfaErmLerL

**4**

## SOMEWHERE
## RAINBOW

**5**

Pict res

**6**

MAUD

**7**

# RASINGINGIN

**8**

**9**

# WHENYOUWISH

# MOVIE PROGRAM

Movie and theater buffs will love this section. These word puzzles are the titles of movies and plays, or phrases or sayings having to do with these forms of entertainment. And . . . roll 'em!

# GONEWIND

# CUCKOONEST

# Good
# Bad

# Ugly

**4**

# Fiddler
# The Roof

---

**5**

| SEASONS | MAN |
|---------|-----|
| SEASONS | MAN |
| SEASONS | MAN |
| SEASONS | MAN |

---

**6**

# NOONMIDNIGHT

---

**7**

## MUTINY
## THE BOUNTY

**8**

ado

ado

ado ado ado

ado ado

ado NOTHING ado

ado ado

ado ado ado

ado ado ado ado

**9**

# spri ng

24

R
O
O
M

R T H
 H
E   E
 T A

O
V
A
T
I
O
N

men

men

men

# Snow White

dwarf dwarf dwarf
dwarf dwarf dwarf
dwarf

# NIGHTMARE ELM ST.

# ANIMALS! ANIMALS!

No G K I D, the following
N I D animal word puzzles
are a lot of fun!

27

1.

OWL

2.

grasnakess

3.

Quack Quack
Cluck Cluck

**4**

Str horses eam

**5**

CHICKEN

┌─────────────────────┐
│                     │
└─────────────────────┘

**6**

OINTFLYMENT

**7**

# P<small>MINNOW</small>OND

---

**8**

blue jays     bbb
robins     bbb
sparrows     bbb

---

**9**

# K9
# THE

10

BBBBBBBB

11

mibearnd

12

Your Bonnet

**13**

B
B B B B
B B B B B
B B B B
B B B

**14**

G H O
N 1S R

**15**

# MANDOGGER

# FOOD FOR THOUGHT

Once you get the hang of the next word puzzles, they'll be as easy as pie!

**1**

 MEAL MEAL MEAL DAY

**2**

 doodle

**3**

$$\begin{array}{r} T \\ T \\ + T \\ \hline 3T \end{array}$$

**4**

egg
egg
easy

**5**

SPUDS

**6**

BEAN bean BEAN bean bean

**7**

X
TOAST

**8**

SPIEKY

**9**

T42

*M**IN**ESTRONE*

*SU EY*

*APPLE*

**13**

cookies·ice cream
apple pie·parfait·
lemon meringue pie·
chocolate cake·

**14**

# I SING
# ANGEL FOOD

**15**

ICE ICE ICE
ICE ICE ICE

**16**

GGES   EGSg

GegS   seGG

---

**17**

T
I
M
A
H

---

**18**

NOON T

salad

$$n^o \quad n \quad n^o \quad n \quad n^o \quad n$$
$$o \quad i \quad o \quad i \quad o \quad i$$

# BREAD

# BODY LANGUAGE

**MIBEARND** — a part of your body can be found in each of the following puzzles.

1.

PAT
THE

2.

OUT
LEG

3.

P
NONON A ONONO
Y

# tHE  sAnD

*cry*          *cry*
*SHOULDER*

# HAHATND

**7**

# EKORTS

**8**

# HEARTEN

**9**

on on on on on on on on on on on (arranged in a circle)

# GHLAONVDE

# 11

# PILF

ear ear

**13**

MOUTH

HAND MOUTH

MOUTH

---

**14**

GNIHCAYMO

---

**15**

head
heels

16

**DAB**

17

**nepainck**

18

b
m
u
h
t

b
m
u
h
t

HEAD      SHOULDERS
arms     body     legs
ankles    feet     toes

# DOFOOTOR

faredce

Ci ii

**25**

i
**bag**

i
**bag**

**26**

ㅗ∩WWƛ

**27**

**fighting**

# THE HAND

## RAE    FAED

## NO NO NO RIGHT

**31**

*cheek* *cheek*

**32**

# HEAD

**33**

## GROUND

feet     feet     feet

feet     feet     feet

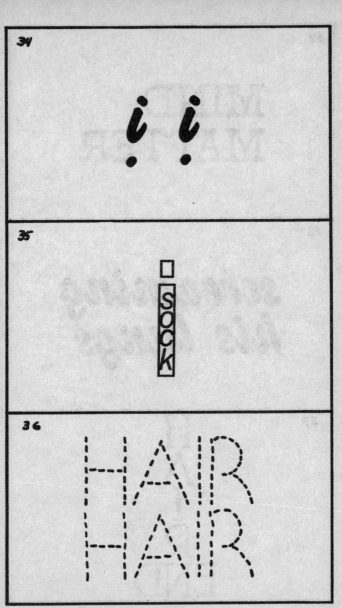

34

35

36

**37**

# MIND
# MATTER

**38**

*screaming
his lungs*

**39**

H
A
I
R
END

# SAY THAT AGAIN

Solve this next section of word tricks and you'll find familiar expressions and figures of speech.

1

*sitting*
*world*

---

2

**SHOT**

---

3

*no one*
*the law*

**4**

better or worse
better or worse
better or worse
better or worse

**5**

BCAUGHTIND

**6**

stone
stone
stone
stone

**7**

*UOY BUR*

**8**

**greenvy**

**9**

**end**
**n**
**d**

**10**

**few farfew**

**11**

**knock timber**

**12**

YOUR HAT
keep it

**13**

EAR

ARE

AREA

EAR

REAR

ARE

**14**

*SKATING*

iiiiiiiiiiii

**15**

hot handle
hot handle

16

*writing*
*wall*

17

L̷E̷AST

18

**R|E|A|D|I|N|G**

61

19

TWOTWO

20

T
THTHROUGHICK
I
N

21

GIVE GET
GIVE GET
GIVE GET
GIVE GET

# 22

LOOK

***blood*** WATER

*home*
*kidney lung heart*

**25**

*safe s**r**o**r**r**y*

**26**

| shape |
| or |

ship

**27**

one another
one another
one another
one another
one another
one another

tahw must

**step   pets   pets**

cry milk

**31**

*bea bush ting*

**32**

**good, better,**

**33**

foot    shoe
foot

34

1.2.3.4.5.6..
THOUGHT

35

cleanlinessgodliness

36

Golden Gate
water

**37**

U
P
U
P
The

**38**

T
LIVE

**39**

WRitING

# ODDS AND ENDS

Here are some more word tricks for you to figure out, but this time you're on your own. We aren't giving you even the slightest clue to help you along!

**EE E**

*(illustration of a bar chart / picket fence beneath the letters)*

Then brackets again leave room for you to have, or
...Then there's room for you to...handsort...and
...see if straight down to the... row along.

**ERA**

**GEN      TION**

*gladglad*
*gladglad*
*gladglad*

strain
a
e
b

# MINDMIND

c
o
m
earth

# momanon

# 5:00 in 6:00

# ZZZZ
# JOB

10

ISOCKT

11

JUST

12

ME

∩

**13**

♡ sight sight

**14**

court

**15**

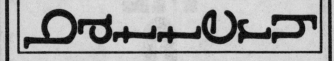

k
c
u
t
s

k
c
u
t
s

word
word
word
word

STAND

I

good  last

good  last

19

**TOE.**

20

**M M**
**A P**

21

**SerUvice**

22

# MIL1LION

23

# J OB

24

*customer*
*customer*
*customer*
*customer*

**25**

down
FARM

**26**

**27**

tistitchme

**28**

*A K Q J*
*Table*

**29**

CROWD   TO

**30**

pa per

**31**

# nine
# cumulus

**32**

# TOUCH

# EARTH

**33**

# LOOKING 1111

## 34

you just me

## 35

**IT** it

## 36

**LOSS**  **word**
**word**
**word**
**word**

*thingthing*

# 38

# BEWARE

40

ENTURY

41

MESS

42

*m*  *o*
*e*  *k*

the morning

# HIS.TORY

**Way**

**Getting**

e s m
k o e s m
k o

# CALL

# PAST

**49**

# Judgøment

**50**

friend
misunderstanding
friend

**51**

*belt*

*hitting*

# CHECK-OUT TIME

How good a word-puzzle solver are you? Here's your chance to find out. The answers to all the word tricks are on the following pages. Check them out.

89

92